~WHO I WAS~WHO I AM~ ~WHO I HAVE BECOME~

~WHO I WAS~WHO I AM~ ~WHO I HAVE BECOME~

LORENZO KEITH

authorHOUSE®

AuthorHouse™ LLC
1663 Liberty Drive
Bloomington, IN 47403
www.authorhouse.com
Phone: 1-800-839-8640

Published by AuthorHouse   12/04/2013

ISBN: 978-1-4918-4047-4 (sc)
ISBN: 978-1-4918-4046-7 (hc)
ISBN: 978-1-4918-4045-0 (e)

Library of Congress Control Number: 2013922138

TABLE OF CONTENTS

DEDICATION

This book is dedicated to Fert and Rachael Morrison Keith who gave all that they had to ensure their children hearts would be fill with the love of God. They raised their children in the "Deep South" at a time when discrimination was the law of the land, depicted by hateful divided words on signs and billboards. This is also dedicated to my eight brothers and three sisters who successfully cared for their family through the good and bad times by the grace of God.

Last, it honors the soldiers and their families whose lives I have inspired by helping them reach their life goals. Above all, it was Myrtle working behind the scenes later in my life serving God and our family simply by being the glue that held the family together. It was my wife's wise counsel over the years that helped me endure life's struggles that came our way.

Myrtle is a very loving person that I salute each day.

"Honour thy father and thy mother, as the Lord thy God hath commanded thee; that thy days may be prolonged, and that it may go well with thee, in the land which the Lord thy God giveth thee." ~Deuteronomy 5:16~

INTRODUCTION

My goal in writing this book is to inspire other work through destructive criticism and hard times; by leaning and depending on Jesus. This book should encourage others to use hateful language as a positive tool to treat others the way you wanted to be treated. Additionally, its design to express what faith can to do when you place it in God. Faith will help you make the right decision in any tasks you are trying to accomplish. Hopefully, this book will keep you focus on being a good citizen willing to serving this great nation and its people.

~ONE~

Who I was: 0-12 years old

"And God said, Let the earth bring forth grass, the herb yielding seed, and the fruit tree yielding fruit after his kind, whose seed is in itself, upon the earth: and it was so." ~Genesis 1:11~

My life story began on August 9, 1951, in Eudora, a little town by in the southeastern corner of the state of Arkansas. The town population is posted at 2,327 to date. I am the proud son of Fert and Rachael Morrison Keith. From what I can remember Mom always made a point to inform me that I was their seventh child. My life during this time was full of poverty, lack of food, clothes; toys, money and plumbing. It was a life of hard work, early rising, and family values that caused my faith to cry out; that God would one day bring an end to hard times.

This faith and hope was taught by my mother without fail to each of her children. She prepared us to survive in a household full of boys by ensuring we all knew how to cook, clean the house, wash clothes and sew. Her teachings, songs and prayers helped to shape the value system of my world then and now, through the good times and bad. Later, I eventually became my mother's trained baker and chief cook in our household in Arkansas.

Being around her ninety percent of the time, I adopted her faith in the awesome power of God. Mom's faith helped shape my spiritual beliefs and it also acted as a foundation for my belief system. I believe every person has a moral right to worship God in spirit and in truth holding on to being free one day. Free from racial division and hateful conservation. Destructed language never accomplishes anything useful in any home setting in America. I held onto the "seventh child" hope that mother passed onto me; God will change things. He always has a timeline to bring about life change that works out for the good of all God's people. Jesus has never failed to answer prayers, calling for relief of pain and suffering of his people. My journey of praising the Almighty God begins with this word; I was inspired by the following Bible's verse:

"Praise God in His sanctuary; praise Him in His mighty Heaven. Praise Him for His acts of power; praise Him for His surpassing greatness." ~Psalm 150: 1-2~

NOTES

G. C. John High School graduate 1970

~TWO~

Praising Almighty God . . .

"Behold, happy is the man whom God correcteth: therefore despise not thou the chastening of the Almighty." ~Job 5:17

PROLOGUE

I praise Him in the morning, the evening and at midnight when I wake up to his voice. Ilearned He is worthy of all our praise whether we give it or not. He is the God of love and the God of our Father's Isaac, Abraham and Jacob. He is the one God who came out of nowhere and said I am going to make me a world. He spoke the word and every living thing was formed and he gave man dominion over every living thing on the face of the Earth. What an awesome God we serve. He's worthy of our praise. He made man in his own image and gave man a soul when he blew into his nostrils the breath of life. What an awesome God he is. His works is done and on the seventh day God rested from labor.

The number seven stays with me in the back of my mind; as I accomplish tasks succeeding at my career goals. It reminds me that God may have a divine path I must take to help others, reminding them of his abiding love for his people. It was clear to me that God will be first in my life decision making process. He would be the one to end the hard times that brought me to my knees many times and made me humble symbolic before God's Throne. As I grew stronger in my core ethic beliefs, the traveled road ahead in life became clearer. The people begin to separate themselves into two groups, the positive and negative. Good and bad was their underlining theme which allowed me to choose my associates. I would choose those who had great work ethic arriving at a positive outcome. I learned that those who embraced poor work ethic always worked overtime achieving nothing. Each would spend huge energy blaming others for their failures. That is why you should always adopt hard work with positive effort.

During the first 12 years of my life, I learned to work hard for three dollars a day from sun up to sun down doing farm work. My father was the only role model I learned from and became my hero and guide on how to survive hard times. My mother taught me how to sustain a spiritual belief that God will always watch over me whether I was rich or poor. Mother knew God like no other person. She was solid as a rock, always telling her children we will make it somehow, achieving a better life. She would always say, "prayer changes things." Mother was right about the power of God as he manifested himself in our family life. Only he could cause food to be on our table when we didn't have a clue where breakfast, lunch and dinner were. Rachael M. Keith, knew the Lord heard and would answer her prayer to feed her family. I adopted that faith because I witnessed the results of an awesome God in action.

Food was provided by a flock of large birds flying over our property landing in the field. I believe that God did that. Food was delivered by heavy rain in the ditch in front of our house filing it with yellow catfish. We were able to fill three number 2 tubs. Lastly, God provided a field that became a breeding ground for rabbits that never ran dry providing meat for our table because of mother Rachael's faith in prayer to a loving God. She made sure the love of God would be instilled in our hearts for all people even those who meant us harm. She called for prayer because she believed they were lost and someone must pray for the haters. She knew once prayer is evoked, God will do the rest to fix what was wrong every time. I became a true prayer warrior in every organization that employed me.

"I know the thoughts that I think toward you," says the Lord, *"thoughts of peace and not of evil, to give you a future and a hope." ~Jeremiah 29:11~*

NOTES

~THREE~

God Gave Me Peace
in My Heart . . .

"The Lord shall fight for you, and ye shall hold your peace."

~Exodus 14:14~

God has never wished man any harm. He has given man the best of his love. He knew when he made man he would need a savior. Man has realized he can do nothing without the will of God. God allows things to happen through his permissive will and invokes his divine will when man continues his defiant ways. God would rather man obey him by choice by worshipping him because it is the right thing to do, showing God that man loves him. It will also show God that man is willing to do as God commands him to do which is love one another. It is hopeful that one day mankind will reach his full potential of love for the Lord Jesus Christ. It's clear that God loves us based on all that he does because He allows our lives to continue despite our rebellious ways. God has extended an olive branch to mankind from Genesis to Revelation hoping one day we will worship him in spirit and in truth. Each year we as a people renew our faith in God; lend a helping hand to others when natural disaster strikes our shores, cities and communities. Psalm of David states:

"I will bless you as long as I live; in your name I will lift up my hands." ~Psalm 63:4~

NOTES

~FOUR~

God is in The Blessing Business . . .

"And I will make of thee a great nation, and I will bless thee and make thy name great; and thou shalt be a blessing."
~Genesis 12:2~

When we are able to get up in the morning and lift up holy hands to the Heaven above, it is because of God's love for us. When we breathe in fresh air it's because of God. When we feel a need to pray each and every day it is all about God on the inside of us. His love is greater than the followers of Moses; greater than Abraham, Isaac, and Jacob's love for their people. One writer said his love is sufficient for me. His love heals all, his love cures all pain and his love is the greatest love of all. His love will make you lift us his name just as Jesus was lifted on the cross of Calvary to bare the sins of the world on his shoulders. He shed his blood washing our sin away. Jesus has blessed me with great teachers that embrace His everlasting love.

From age 6 to 12, my teachers became educational role models in my life as my world began to broaden outside the walls of our three room home. I have had too many teachers to name, but they taught me how to become a team player, team leader and a team follower. My teachers introduced me to the world of continuing education. In the teacher's arena, I began to exercise my brain by exploring the subject Math, learning about other countries, and different cultures. It developed a hunger inside of me to visit other parts of the world. My teachers caused me to dream of a world that was seen in my vision; free from racial insults, hatred, and confinement inside the walls of our home in Eudora, Arkansas.

One cannot imagine that my world was full of hatred by a group of individuals who placed no limits on themselves. I woke up every day to insulting words directed at me because I was a different skin color. If you weren't saved by God spiritually you could have ended up hating those who call you awful names. I needed help to overcome that culture in Eudora, Arkansas. My teachers opened my mind to learn about a world where all people could be free from insults. There were those who taught me to use hateful insults which in turn became a motivation to work overtime to be successful. Later in life, it was so clear this was the Lord molding and shaping me. I had to adapt to around non—loving people. It was a challenge in the beginning and throughout the years made me less tolerant of hateful language. Many times I made a decision to put an end to it very quickly without regards of consequences.

Whether these things are Right or wrong, your mindset concludes there is no room for hateful people in this twenty first century. That is why I thank God for those teachers introducing me to a world full of hope. Dreams do make a difference in a world where hope is alive and shared by so many positive people of God. Dreams brought me closer to understand God presence in my life; it enlightens me to His works to change man's ability to display love. His spiritual presence kept me from giving up on my lost brothers and sister ability to do God's will which is to love one another. I prayed many mornings and nights to remain focused in carrying out the will of God. What I was experiencing in my life made me depend on God's word from the book of Matthew:

"Come to Me, All of you who are weary and carry heavy burdens, and I will give you rest." ~Matthew 11:28~

NOTES

~FIVE~

God is a Burden Bearer . . .

"Wherefore say unto the children of Israel, I am the Lord, and will bring you out from under the burdens of the Egyptians, and I will rid you out of their bondage, and I will redeem you with a stretched arm, and with great judgments." ~Exodus 6:6~

God, through his love for us will give us rest if we come to accept him. He is a burden bearer and a way maker. God wants us to depend on him to lead us to glory: up in his Kingdom where there will be no more pain, no more worry and no more hunger. Jesus died and rose again so that we have a right to the tree of life. He paid the price for all who accept him as their personal savior. He will come into our heart and sup with us (give us rest). When God gives you rest, it involves great joy. When God gives you rest his love swells your heart, leaving no room for hatred. When hatred is gone from your heart you begin thanking God for His unconditional love that makes dreams possible.

My dreams were constant. They were real and full of hope that the God of Heaven would free all people from the evil spirit of hatred flowing over the land. The air in America was not flowing with opportunities for all Americans. My mother's voice was a driving force in my heart and mind reminding me of God's unconditional love for his people. It encourages me to never lose faith knowing that a brighter day is coming because of his grace. My mother's voice never let me pick up the evil tool of hate for another. Mother had a forgiving heart and gave part of it to me. She knew Jesus sits on the right hand side of God's throne and he command us to love one another. He asks the Father to forgive us for we know not what we do. Between my mother and teachers, I was able to emerge with the love of God in my heart instead of hate and deceitfulness. This bible verse tells me to cry out for God peace:

~May the lord of Peace Himself give you peace at all times and in every way. ~ 2 Thessalonians 3:16. ~

NOTES

~SIX~

How Powerful is God's Peace . . .

"Now the God of hope fill you with all the joy and peace in believing, that ye may abound in hope, through the power of the Holy Ghost." ~Romans 15:13~

As I cried out to the Lord for His peace, I found it's great for my soul salvation. I will always need the Lord to continue to fill me with his peace. Now I can see things clearly from the umbrella of God's love hovering over me. My soul cried out for His love and glory to be with me every day. I know I love the lord, for He alone provides me comfort in the mist of confusion. It was God who helped me survive the hateful times of my life. He loves me for who I am and He's not through with me yet. I pray that the Lord's peace stay with me as I travel life's highway doing His will.

God's peace will always comfort me. It has and always will give me strength to walk by faith and praise my Lord. It's clear God's love and peace is sufficient for me. Lord I thank you for your love and mercy in my life plus my teacher's mindset to explain your love to their students.

NOTES

~SEVEN~

Who I am: 13 to 19 years old . . .

"And God said unto Moses, I AM That I AM: and he said, Thus shalt thou say unto the children of Israel, I AM hath sent me unto you." ~Exodus 3:14~

My teachers introduced me to the preaching, and teaching of Dr. Martin Luther King, a value system that would shape my life today. It was during this time period that I learned more about the history of mankind and who I am than any period of my life. It was my teachers whose tears and emotions at the death of Dr. King, made me understand why love for one another must become the overriding factor to achieve racial harmony among the people of the world. The worlds view from my eyes was full of racial hatred and limited opportunities for a young black man growing up in rural Arkansas. Our white brothers and sisters assaulted us with many racial insults reflecting the cruelty of their hearts. I used to think there was no love of God in their hearts for anyone but themselves.

However, my mother and teachers cleared that up right away. I was informed that love and hatred cannot coexist in the same heart. As a human being you will either love one another or you will choose to hate. It is because the Almighty God made our heart to be a united form of humanity so we cannot serve two masters at the same time. Reality says you can't love your family and hate your neighbors. One must fill their heart with the emotion of hate or love.

Once I put some thoughts into my teachers reality check; it all made sense for me. It takes a lot of rage to store up hatred in your heart and it is difficult to shed in order to have a loving relationship with your family in a home setting. Life tells me that a person that displays harmful emotion lives a miserable life. Therefore, someone has to be able to pray for their soul salvation in God's Kingdom.

In listening to those educators, I adopted the title as a *Prayer Warrior* for others who failed to realize they were standing in the need of prayer. Being a Prayer Warrior helped build my character and made me focus on allowing the Lord's Holy Spirit to work in my life as well as in others. It made me understand that God alone can bring about an emotional event to change the hearts of people to love. When reading this verse I ask the Lord to create a clean heart for me:

~Create in me a clean heart, O God, and renew a steadfast spirit within me. ~ Psalm 51: 10~

NOTES

~EIGHT~

A Clean Heart
Works Better . . .

"Create in me a clean heart, O God; and renew a right spirit within me." ~Psalm 51:10~

Inspired by the Holy Spirit, I asked the Lord to create in me a clean heart so I could embrace His peace. I felt the need to embrace God's love in my daily life so I could continue to do His will. When I embraced my clean heart He filled me with the Holy Spirit. He became and still is the Comforter that Christ spoke of with his disciples; before he left Earth to sit on the right hand side of God's Throne. He removed all ungodly emotions from my heart allowing me to treat everybody right. This enables me to treat people the way I want to be treated. My teachers helped me find that clean heart mindset. It was the clean heart God gave me that secured my family stability.

I further learned that family values would merge with those from my teachers; to influence my way of thinking, decision making process, and my way of life. The process used by these teachers at G.C. John School in Eudora elevated my self-esteem as a young person living in a small town with limited knowledge of the world around me. Somehow, I began to realize things happened in my world for a reason; which led me to believe that I was put here by God to make a difference in people's lives. Many people I encountered needing help would be a stranger to me, seeking my advice. It was through those people's lives that my life's dream became real and no longer a vision.

All of my small town education was encouraging me to go further into the world and get involved in finding my destiny. My Father's voice was telling me to follow in his footsteps and become a soldier. As my draft number dropped to one, fate took its course and I volunteered for the army draft on April 29, 1972. At that moment, I entered into the United States army to become a professional soldier.

It was at Fort Knox that my real life transformation from a civilian to a young combat soldier began. On July 12, 1972, 300 hundred soldiers including myself were placed on an airplane to later learn we were heading to Vietnam. Fate would have the pilot announce the plane was being rerouted to Wichita Airbase in Kansas. When we heard the news over the public announcement system we were stunned. No soldiers uttered a word; we all realized God had his hand in that decision. It was complete silence from me and the soldiers in route to Wichita Airbase. We arrived at the hanger guarded by military policemen that was enclosed by entangled barb wires. It was there we spent two week of our lives before riding Greyhound buses to Fort Riley, Kansas.

NOTES

~NINE~

Who I will Become: 20 to 29 and Beyond . . .

"And the Lord God said, Behold, the man is become as one of us, to know good and evil: and not, lest he put forth his hand, and take also of the tree of life, and eat, and live forever."
~Genesis 3:22~

During this time period, the army taught me a "new language" with English words I hadn't heard before such as: squad leader, platoon sergeant, first sergeant and sergeant major. It added words as duty, honor and country to my vocabulary. I began to echo more words like loyalty, integrity, duty, honor, selfless service and personal courage. Later I learned each word had a lifetime commitment with its meaning that started a new way of life for me. I would soon use those new terms to sustain my body while and soul conducting my nation's business in harm's way. The most important people in my life became my military leaders, teachers, and spiritual leaders at home and abroad.

Note: Through the transformation of my early life, the people who supported me the most were my family. They always said the sky was the limit for career success. My family reminded me to never quit and use destructive criticism on anyone. That advice served as my conscience in life.

The duties of a soldier became the turning point of my life's mission. I knew then that God wanted me to become a professional soldier. It was then that I selected small volume books to read about. The books were titled, *Military Tactics* by George S. Patton and *The Lost art of War* by SUN TZU II. These two military warriors would surge my energy in training soldiers for the greatest army on the face of the Earth. When faced with overwhelming odds, these leaders never accepted defeat, but drew upon a higher calling to give them the wisdom to win the battle at hand. Their principle of leadership and concept for training became my training tools to mold and shape the minds of army soldiers. Therefore, it was clear to me that I would spend the next three decades of my life fighting our nation's battles on the modern battlefield anytime and anywhere. I refused none.

The life of a soldier became my dreams, goals, and prayers. I prayed that God would always allow me to be trained and ready to deploy within 24 hours. That meant I could go anywhere in the world if my nation called upon me to do so. This kind of commitment wasn't a part of my life's motivation until I entered into training with the US Army. Not only did the army instill in within me the dedication to duty, it made this old soldier a committed father, husband and a great citizen of this country. I became a self-appointed ambassador to the US Army while deployed overseas. Anything I said or did would reflect greatly upon the soldiers, US Army and United States of America.

However, my challenges came when trying to influence other soldiers to share that same commitment; to honor the culture different of the host country while serving. That was a responsibility that I took very serious with everyone under my span of control. Additionally, I believe my greatest accomplishment was leading a group of soldiers into three major battles while never losing a soldier. That was an incredible feeling of relief and a display of the awesome power by God.

These experiences taught me to be humble in my decision making and show compassion when dealing with the problems of others. Being a soldier inspired me to serve this country by encouraging others to enter into the continuing education process and also to help our nation's children reach their goals. That is why I am a life member of the following military organizations: The association of US Army (AUSA), Noncommissioned Officer Association (NCOA), The Retired Enlisted Association (TREA), and Veteran of Foreign Wars (VFW). Also, I am a life member of the National Infantry Association (NIA), Noncommissioned Officer Museum at Ft. Bliss Texas and a member of American Legion.

The professional organizations listed in the above paragraph support and provide aid for service member's family. Those organizations have inspired me to set my goals for the next five years. I believe that setting goals plays an important part in the life of retired soldiers and their families by fighting for our benefits.

NOTES

~TEN~

First Five Year Plan . . .

"And he shall be like a tree planted by the rivers of water, that bringeth forth his fruit in his season; his leaf also shall not wither; and whatsoever he doeth shall prosper." ~Genesis 3:22~

~MY FIRST FIVE YEAR PLAN~

My first five year plan is outlined below:
WHO I HAVE BECOME

November 2004-May 2005

I will graduate from Webster University with honor and be a committed alumnus to support the University goals. This means helping future students coming out of our nation military to continue the education process with Webster University.

June 2005-December 2005

I will work hard to be employed at Limestone College and continue to support the college alumnus. It is my dream to stay connected to my undergraduate alumni continuing education process by recruiting others and teaching at the BlockProgram in Columbia South Carolina.

January 2006-December 2007

It is my plan to become a life member in five civilian organizations that is involved in helping children. These organizations must be committed to the mental, spiritual and physical growth of our nation's youth.

January 2007-December 2008

It's my desire and commitment to continue to serve my country on land, air and sea. That means, continuing to support the men and women in uniforms as they deploy around the world doing our nation's business. It also means to keep my life membership in military associations active in voting for future benefits for our country Veterans and their family.

January 2008-December 2009

During this year I will start planning for my final retirement home in the state of South Carolina. Additionally I will, dedicate my life energy in becoming an effective motivational speaker for our nations young who needs encouragement.

The above five year plan will work for me because; I am committed to serve God, country and others. It is something I have done all of my life and believed it is the most noble service during peace time. It is Christ who commands me to love one another. This command has engrained itself into my spirit and became the driving force behind my life goals. In five years I will stay on track praying for wisdom to know the right opportunities to join five civilian organizations that help children. <u>That will be my sign of continued service.</u>

NOTES

~ELEVEN~

Second Five Year Plan . . .

"And he shall be like a tree planted by the rivers of water, that bringeth forth his fruit in his season; his leaf also shall not wither; and whatsoever he doeth shall prosper." ~Genesis 3:22~

~MY SECOND FIVE YEAR PLAN~

My second five year plan
is outlined below:
WHO I WILL BECOME

*I will continue with plan to pay off our Mortgage that is under the four year mark-reaching that goal. The line items below depict my current five year plan for the Keith' Foundation:

- (1). My five year plan begins with: *October 2013 through October 2014*: I Plan to finish my second book and send it to the publisher at Author house.
  *October 2013: The goal is to place my manuscript in the hand of a typist for first edit. The focus is to complete the second book manual script and its second edit by December 2013.

- (2).*November 2014—November 2015*: Hopefully, complete the publishing process and purchase the first 250 books for a book signing in 2015. Ensure the book has a blue outer cover or dominant outline <u>cover border in blue.</u>
  *Continue to pray for the safety of this country poorest people and the President of the United States.

- (3).*December 2015 through December 2016*: Have another book signing event in a new state at a military base.
  *Continue to plan another book signing event with friends in the future.
  *Encourage others to vote in the President election in 2016.

- (4). *January 2017 through December 2018*:
  *Finalize plan on land and a new home at the affordable market price.

*Continue in prayer for our nation sincere leadership to do God will for our nation people.

*Take the dream vacation for our forty year anniversary.

My current five year plan is on track to be a success story. The second book process has begun. The goals of this five year plan and events will be met and many people will be inspired by its easy read and the inspiring thoughts. It is clear to me that life does not wait on anyone to succeed. One must become a visionary and develop a realistic plan that is workable. That plan must be acted upon with workable resources based on a fixed income.

As an individual you will come to many crossroads in your life's journey. Your job is to choose the right path that will lead you to a successful life. No one can do it alone, we all need help. Therefore, we must always pray to God for his wisdom and understanding. He alone will inspire you to do what is right. In the midst of turmoil God will see you through. No task will over power you with the Lord on your side. He will inspire you to stay focused on solving problems the right way and he is always on time. I never lost sight of the values that allowed me to help others in this great nation.

Always remember your ability to serve will become your greatest strength for success in life as you face challenges. Never feel that God has abandoned you in your quest to become a productive citizen in the United States of America. The Lord is always near in time of trouble and closer in your joyous moments. Clearly, God is a spirit; one must worship him in spirit and truth. A word from the Prophet Isaiah encourages us to sing with joy; to the God of Heaven.

"Sing for joy, O heavens, and exult, O earth; break forth, O mountains, into singing! For the Lord has comforted His people. Isaiah 49: 40: 13"~

NOTES

~TWELVE~

Why Sing to the Lord . . .

"Hear, O ye kings; give ear, O ye princes; I, even I, will sing unto the Lord; I will sing praise to the Lord God of Israel."
~Judges 5:3~

Truly God has blessed man since the beginning of time. Isaiah called on the heavens and earth to sing with great joy for the Lord is worthy. The reason you should sing to God is because of the creation of his hands. Also, look at what He has done for his people since the beginning of time. He made the Heavens and Earth. I have learned the Lord's will be done on Earth as it is in Heaven. God will take care of us, because He loves us.

We should sing for all the darkest hours on Earth, God will replace with peace. Especially, when it appears mankind was set for self-destruction. We must praise Him for whom all our blessing flows. His presence is seen in the trees, wind and the rain. I sing praises to him for all he has done in my life; his quiet voice early in the morning comforts me in my spirit. When I call on him he is always there leaving me with his abiding peace. As we approach the holiday seasons I feel inspired to share what God has laid upon my heart as the seventh child.

NOTES

~THIRTEEN~

My Inspired Thoughts . . .

"O Lord, how great are thy works! And thy thoughts are very deep." ~Psalm 92:5~

The holiday season is upon us once again. God has seen fit to allow us to see year 2013 grow closer to an end. It is my prayer that all people will look to the mighty God for strength, wisdom, and guidance to get them through year 2014. We are not to look towards the politicians who believe they know what's best for mankind. It hurts my head to think that they believe we as a people are too stupid to recognize who loves us and who doesn't. It is a sad day in this world when elected officials have no care or concern about the amount of lies and the amount of pain they have caused people of this world who have worked their rear end off to make ends meet. No matter how hard the people work, the more debt occurs and the higher the taxes. Only in America can the elected official stay in office for due process of the law until their term expires.

We as a people must pray that one day our lost and well educated leaders will see the pain and suffering they have inflicted on the poor people of the nation. Lord helps us if they can't hear. Lord helps us if they never see. Lord helps us if they look the other way and conduct business as usual.

NOTES

~FOURTEEN~

Which Way Are
You Going . . .

*"And, behold, this day I am going the way of all the earth: and
ye know in all your hearts and in all your souls that not one
thing hath failed of all the good things which the Lord your
God spake concerning you; all are come to pass unto you, and
not one thing hath failed thereof." ~Joshua 23:14~*

We travel many roads in our life path. Some lead to challenges that cause great pain and misery to us and sometimes others. The way of life's path isn't always clear and many times full of obstacles too steep to climb without a helping hand and much prayer.

One thing for sure you must travel in order to get ahead in your life's goals. You must travel to move with time, or time will pass and leave you with many unanswered questions. You must travel to explore the pools of knowledge that lie ahead of you in many culture backgrounds. Stay on your life's path, if the roadway is breeding success. Work hard at a common goal; mean performing. Never doubt your own ability and capability. Give God the glory regardless if you succeed. Surely he allowed you to be a winner. Ask nothing of yourself; accept a level playing field to work your heart out. Never complain about the process being unfair, just recognize what it is and keep pushing to complete the mission.

Be the master at making peace. Set the example of being a team player of high integrity. Remember it is not about you, it is about God in your life. Now which way do I go in life? That is my question.

NOTES

~FIFTEEN~

What is Man . . .

"So God created man in his own image, in the image of God created he him; male and female created he them." ~Genesis 1:27~

Man is said to be a reflection of God himself; a creation of God. Man is said to be made a little lower than the angels. He is crowned with glory and honor. Man is said to have dominion over every living thing in the air, on the land, and in the seas. Man is said to be the reason why Christ came out of his heavenly place to live among us on earth. The very existence of man seems to indicate that God will always be present here on earth to take care of humanity. It appeared that God wants man to succeed in all that he does. It appears that man cannot fail if he puts God first in all that he plans to do. The question remains; what is man? He is a creature of faith. Man is a fountain of ideas. He is a temple of worship. Man is a carrier of the word of the almighty God. The Lord has asked man since the beginning of time to do two things; one of which is greater than all them. First he must worship the Lord thy God with all his heart, soul and mind. Secondly, he must love one another all the days of his life. So is man a creature of Love ordained by God to show love for one another? Can man overcome some of his evil ways and surrender himself unto God's will? There is hope for humanity. The word of God never fails to protect mankind.

NOTES

~SIXTEEN~

Our Words Are a Bond . . .

"And these words, which I command thee this day, shall be in thine heart." ~Deuteronomy 6:6~

Words of man are powerful and represent the essence of a man. If man is to survive, he must keep his word is all that he do. Man's word builds character and establishes bonds one to another. I believe the word of a man represents his soul intention. God spoke the word before the beginning of time. In speaking of his word a generation was formed. Man himself was created by God himself in his own image; in Gods likeness. The word was God himself. The word was later made flesh and dwelt among us. We behold his glory; full of grace and truth.

Words through the course of time have made peace, started wars and through the course of time have brought nations together to achieve a common goal.

Jesus said man cannot live by bread alone, but by every word that precede out of the mouth of God. Man is the greatest of God's creation. God gave man charge over all living things.

So I say to man-give your word today and live by it for years to come. In the eyes of many, your words will be your bond. Be proud of who you are and where you are going in life and keep your word for all to see.

NOTES

~SEVENTEEN~

What to Be in Life . . .

"He that overcometh, the same shall be clothed in white raiment; and I will not blot out his name out of the book of life, but I will confess his name before my Father, and before his angels." ~Revelations 3:5~

~WHAT TO BE IN LIFE~

{ } Law Enforcement
{ } Educated
{ } Humble
{ } Peace Maker
{ } Good follower
{ } Great Leader
{ } Faithful Disciples
{ } A Good Steward
{ } Prayer Warrior

NOTES

~EIGHTEEN~

Enforce The Law . . .

"And thou shalt teach them ordinances and laws, and shalt shew them the way wherein they must walk, and the work that they must do." ~Exodus 18:20~

Laws are in place to help the government; to control the will of man so the people can survive. Laws are rules that force people to respect the rights of others. When one is trying to decide which law to follow, one must remember what Jesus said. Render unto Caesar that which is Caesar's. Render unto God that which is God's. God's law is the very foundation of man's law. The law lets man know that the final seat of authority lies with God almighty. It is a final check and balance to help man enforce the law without total corruption. Each one of us must face God at his judgment seat before we enter into the kingdom of heaven.

Many may say how can we know the right way to heaven? Jesus said, I am the way, the truth and the light and no man come unto the Father but by me. All you have to do is obey God's law and worship him. He wants you and me to follow ten simple rules of his Law:

{ }Thou shalt have no other god before me.

{ }Thou shalt not make unto thee any graven Image.

{ }Thou shalt not take the name of the Lord thy God in vain.

{ }Remember the Sabbath day, to keep it holy.

{ }Honor thy father and thy mother.

{ }Thou shalt not kill.

{ }Thou shalt not commit adultery.

{ }Thou shalt not steal.

{ }Thou shalt not bear false witness.

{ }Thou shalt not covet.

~Ex 20: 3-17~

God needs holy leaders who are committed to lead his followers out of darkness by the marvelous less light; which is Jesus Christ our Lord. I learned to follow the Lord's leading; he has never failed me yet.

NOTES

~NINETEEN~

The Need of God's Leaders . . .

"Behold, I have given him for a witness to the people, a leader and commander to the people." ~Isaiah 55:

4 ~

Today's leaders in tomorrow's world have to be more creative and more aware of his or her surroundings. It is good that a leader who has been placed in charge of many people's livelihood has prepared him/her for that position of great responsibility. However, many organizations place their leaders in positions because of friendship and not based on the ability to get the job done.

This kind of practice is called OJT which is "on the job training". This concept often brings misery to the work force and continues with confusion. It creates power struggles up and down the chain of command. Many times you will often here the phrase, "who is in charge of this mess".

I say to you that today's leaders must be proactive and not reactive to the needs of the work place. Know your personal strengths and weaknesses so you can best utilize them to make the mission happen.

Do your best to establish a can-do spirit in all of the team members. Many times a great leader develops a "follow me" approach to leading his or her team to productivity in the work place. This style of leadership has been proven to be effective in all stress related environment. Subordinates see leaders in a "follow me" role and usually have a "look at me" type role of leadership.

Leaders of today's world must be aggressive in attacking the missions that are handed to his or her section. This "attacking" style of leadership shows subordinates a willing and able leader that wants to accomplish the job. This kind of high energy is very healthy for an organization. Leaders must work hard at creating this kind of healthy energy that his or her company needs to make it run more effectively.

Team leaders today are saying it is easier to determine what the needs are within an organization but harder to fix it. Some are asking where you begin to foster or create the type of command climate in an organization that fixes problems. My counsel to you is very simple.

To create a good command climate in your organization as a leader; you must fix your attitude first. Always start at home and spread outward. You have to change the way you do business first; let others see that change in a positive light. Only then can the positive change affect others in your organization areas. When you want change to occur you have to lead the team through the process; become the salesperson setting the example.

Never approach change with a negative thought and expecting the mission to happen. It requires solid leadership at all times.

Remember tomorrow is a day that the Lord has made for all of us to call on Him for guidance. He alone has inspired me to speak out about the season of truth that Jesus plays in our lives. It is a season of reality.

NOTES

~TWENTY~

A Season for Jesus . . .

"Then I will give you rain in due season, and the land shall yield her increase, and the trees of the field shall yield their fruit." ~Leviticus 26:4~

In a season of my life I began to see the reality of who Jesus is, what he did, and the reasons he came to Earth. I believe that this helped shape my world to this day. This is the season to be thankful for what God has given to mankind. He has given man his greatest gift; His only son so the world could be saved.

In the city of David a savior was born of the virgin woman named Mary. Here God expressed his love for man that would be talked about for over two thousand years. It was the birth of this spectacular savior, given the name that at the sound of name; every knee will bow and every tongue will confess. At the name of Jesus demons tremble in fear of His awesome powers. In my journey through life with all its ups and downs I learned to praise His name.

The question is, "Can we as a nation continue to be great if we the people don't turn from their wicked ways?" One may say it's hard to measure the full extent of God's love. You may say it's hard to place a limit on His love for man. Yet, it's clear that God loves man with great emotion through our obedient and disobedient days.

Many times we forget to say thank you Lord for all the things that He has done for us. I find myself often at that crossroad in my life. There are times in life where I have been brought me to my knees to praise Him for his "Amazing Grace". The question we need to know the answer to is, "What price will God pay for people's salvation?" Is there a limitation on His love for us? What will be his ultimate sacrifice? I believe we can say it was that day on Calvary when Jesus hung His head and died for the atonement of our sins. God gave the life of His only son, that we might have a right to the tree of life. From the story of Jesus death through the resurrection; I learned to lean and depend on Him for all answers in a complex web of lies in this world.

NOTES

~TWENTY ONE~

Real Truth about Jesus . . .

"Jesus saith unto him, I am the way, the truth, and the life: no man cometh unto the Father, but by me." ~John 14:6~

The bible tell us: "God sent not his son into the world to condemn it, but that the world through Him might be save". ~John 3-17~. The word does not indicate a weakness in Jesus Armor. It means man still has a choice to choose whether he will follow after the example of Christ or perish at the hands of his own actions. God is a giving God. He is a loving God. He is a merciful God. He is a loving God. He is a prayer hearing God. Yet, through it all, he is a God of vengeance. Vengeance is mine saith the Lord. Yet his mercy endures forever. That is why he is called the "Great I AM", the beginning and the ending of all time. He is the Alpha and the Omega. My God is a good God in all that he says and does. Heaven and earth shall pass away, but his word shall not pass away. Jesus said, man cannot live by bread alone, but by every word that precedes out of the mouth of God. The gospel writer remind us, that God so loved the world, that he gave his only begotten son, that whosoever believes in him shall not perish but have everlasting life. God has worked hard to make sure that man knows his plan and the way to his kingdom. Jesus told Thomas, that He was the way the truth and the light, no man comes unto the Father but by him. He has assured us that in his Father's house there are many mansions, if it was not so he would have told us so. Jesus added that He will go to prepare a place for us, that where he is there we will be also.

NOTES

Ft. Jackson BCT 2013 Hilton Field Pvt Keith

~TWENTY TWO~

Jesus is the Way . . .

"Jesus saith unto him, I am the way, the truth, and the life: no man cometh unto the Father, but by me." ~John 14:6~

We as a family must understand the real meaning of Christmas this season. It is not about Santa Claus, it is not about you. It is about God, who alone gave His only begotten son to the world for the ultimate sacrifice so that we as a people would have a right to the tree of life. That tree is located in his Heavenly places. Christmas is about God giving his all, his love, to the world to save it. He knew before the beginning of time that man would need a savior. Man needed Jesus to come into the world to show us the way.

God knew the desires of man's heart and soul. He laid out a plan to sustain and eventually save man from his iniquity. God knew as long as man was allowed to live; his sins would be great before his throne.

So let us give according to God's will. Let us give as our heart desires to. Let us give willingly because it is the right thing to do. Let us give not grudgingly nor of necessity, for God loves a cheerful giver.

NOTES

~TWENTY THREE~

Making a Difference . . .

"And that ye may put difference between holy and unholy, and between unclean and clean." ~Leviticus 10:10~

My mother and teachers made a difference in my life. My value base came from them in their teachings throughout my life. There are many positive role models I can call upon that inspired me to strive for moral excellence when I thought of just giving up. They will always be my hero and in my memory recall bank of knowledge.

You can make a difference in someone's life by simply being very kind with your daily greeting. You can make a difference by giving a word of praise for something you caught someone doing right. It is easy to find fault in other people. It doesn't take a rocket scientist to be able to point out the short comings in others. The word of God tells us we all have sinned and fallen short of the glory of God. You make a difference by uplifting one another, encouraging each other and supporting each team member to accomplish their goals. This will make a difference in the total unit mission accomplishment. You can never have unit cohesions until you work toward having team work, spiritual fitness, and a command climate that lives and breathes equal opportunity for all.

The effective units have the real leader setting the tone and enforcing the standard that allows unit ministry and the equal opportunity to flourish and glow in the organization.

You, as a member of a team have to totally commit and believe that through your hard work and dedication to high moral excellence you can and will make a difference. Making a difference means preparing to do hard work. Making a difference is being willing to have an open mind to hear the concerns of others. Making a difference is being a role model for others and living up to God's Ten Commandments. You can make a difference by letting your life shine as a road map for others to pattern their life after. Your life is a witness to others during the good and bad times.

When will you know that you have truly made a difference in the lives of others; in the organization as a whole? You will know by the gleam in the eyes of others you come in contact with. You will know by the pride displayed by team members to ensure moral excellence and missions happen. You will know by the diversity in your unit coming together willingly to achieve a common goal with personal pride unifying and leading the way. Make a difference by keeping God first in all that you say and do. Put your efforts in treating all people the way you want to be treated. Last, make a difference by giving freely to help someone whose need is greater than yours.

Life has taught me to care about others who are having a difficult time making a living. My Journey in the military has made me humble and respectful to the right of others. I have learned to honor my teachers from Eudora, Arkansas because they opened my eyes to a world full of positive people. My teachers knew I would form bonds and gain knowledge in many cultures around the world. I would learn the world does have good human beings and its share of haters. But it was up to me to choose what kind of man I wanted to be. I chose to walk with God and be inspired by Him to share his plan for salvation.

In this book I added many of my inspired writings that the spirit of the Lord gave me to share with others. I found myself being used by God for his will by delivering messages to group of people. They have gathered to hear what God's word was saying about their lives. As you read this book I pray that you see how my thought process evolves in many writing styles. It allows me to communicate the lessons learned from a hateful environment that I grew up in. It demonstrated what God did to protect me from being filled with hate. He inspired me to tell the world about his plan for salvation. He inspired me to talk about Jesus with a passion unmatched by other.

NOTES

Master Sergeant Deborah Pleasant

Sgt. Meriwether, Sgt. Keith, Sgt. Moore
South Korea 1971